Crazy Cars

Craig A. Lopetz

TABLE OF CONTENTS

What Are Crazy Cars?.............2

Glossary................................23

Index 23

A Crabtree Seedlings Book

What Are Crazy Cars?

Crazy cars are **artist** drawings.

Some are drawn with **airbrush** paints.

Some are drawn on a computer.

Some are painted with crazy colors.

Some crazy cars **pop** their wheels high.

There are old crazy trucks.

There are new crazy trucks.

There are short crazy cars.

Crazy cars have big **motors**.

Real Cars and Crazy Cars

Pontiac GTO

Cadillac Eldorado

Ford Mustang

Glossary

airbrush (AIR-brush): An airbrush is a tool that sprays paint.

artist (AR-tist): An artist is someone who is very good at drawing, painting, or making things.

motors (MOH-turz): Car motors are engines, or machines, that give cars their power.

pop (PAHP): To pop your wheels is to make them jump by revving the motor really hard before releasing the clutch pedal.

Index

artist   2
colors   4, 7
crazy trucks   12, 15
motors   20
paints   2, 7

School-to-Home Support for Caregivers and Teachers

This book helps children grow by letting them practice reading. Here are a few guiding questions to help the reader build his or her comprehension skills. Possible answers appear here in red.

Before Reading
- **What do I think this book is about?** I think this book is about crazy and wild cars. I think this book is about drawings of hot rod cars.
- **What do I want to learn about this topic?** I want to learn more about the different pictures that are drawn on crazy cars. I want to learn how long it takes to draw a crazy car.

During Reading
- **I wonder why...** I wonder why some crazy cars pop their wheels high. I wonder why it's popular to draw flames on crazy cars.

- **What have I learned so far?** I have learned that crazy cars can be short or long. I have learned that crazy cars have big motors usually in the front.

After Reading
- **What details did I learn about this topic?** I have learned that crazy cars are drawn to look like real cars. I have learned that some crazy cars are drawn on a computer and others are drawn with airbrush paints.
- **Read the book again and look for the glossary words.** I see the word *airbrush* on page 2, and the word *pop* on page 3. The other glossary words are found on page 23.

Library and Archives Canada Cataloguing in Publication

CIP available at Library and Archives Canada

Library of Congress Cataloging-in-Publication Data

CIP available at Library of Congress

Crabtree Publishing Company
www.crabtreebooks.com   1-800-387-7650

Written by: Craig A. Lopetz
Print coordinator: Katherine Berti

Print book version produced jointly with Blue Door Education in 2023

Printed in the U.S.A./072022/CG20220201

Content produced and published by Blue Door Education, Melbourne Beach FL USA. This title Copyright Blue Door Education. All rights reserved. No part of this book may be reproduced or utilized in any form or by any means, electronic or mechanical including photocopying, recording, or by any information storage and retrieval system without permission in writing from the publisher.

PHOTO CREDITS:
www.istock.com, www.shutterstock.com. Cover: shutterstock.com | Mechanik. Pages 2-3:shutterstock.com | Mechanik, istock.com | humonia, istock.com | scyther5. Pages 4-5: shutterstock.com | jeffhobrath, shutterstock.com | lazy clouds, shutterstock.com | unicro. Pages 6-7: shutterstock.com | Mechanik, istock.com | natrot. Pages 8-9: shutterstock.com | jeffhobrath, istock.com | sbelov. Pages 10-11: shutterstock.com | Mechanik, istock.com | bennyb. Pages 12-13: shutterstock.com | Mechanik, istock.com | Hennadii. Pages 14-15: shutterstock.com | Mechanik, istock.com | blacklight_trace. Pages 16-17: shutterstock.com | Mechanik, istock.com | Man As Thep. Pages 18-19: istock.com | Mechanik, istock.com | Malchev. Pages 20-21: shutterstock.com | Mechanik, istock.com | Alunal. Pages 22-23: USSource/ford/cadillac.

Published in the United States
Crabtree Publishing
347 Fifth Ave.
Suite 1402-145
New York, NY 10016

Published in Canada
Crabtree Publishing
616 Welland Ave.
St. Catharines, Ontario
L2M 5V6